LEADERSHIP IN TIMES OF CRISIS AND UNCERTAINTY

Guiding Principles for Navigating the Turbulent Waters of Modern Leadership

Pat Bowen

TABLE OF CONTENT

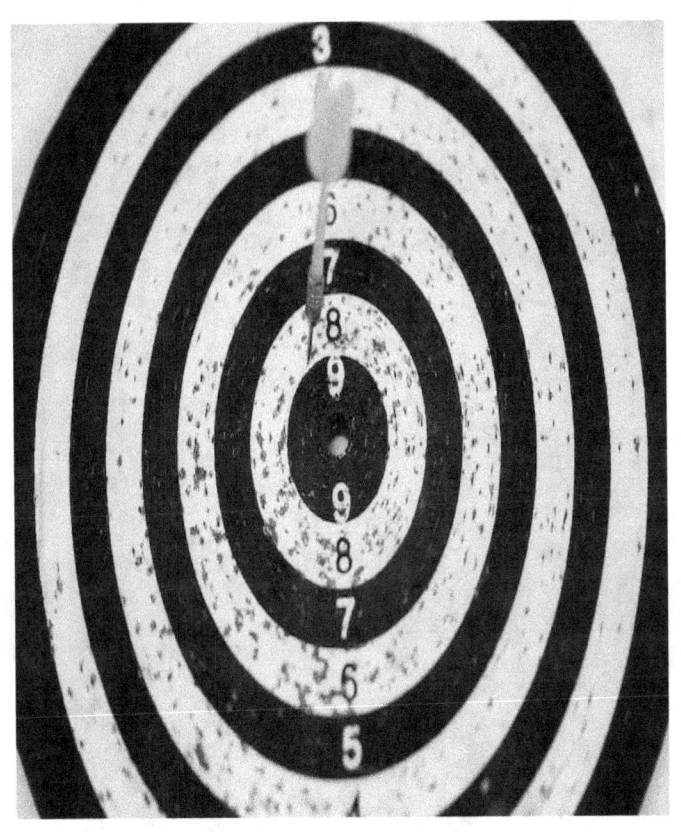

INTRODUCTION

Leadership in times of crisis and uncertainty refers to the ability of individuals or organizations to effectively navigate through turbulent and unpredictable situations. It requires leaders to make critical decisions, inspire and motivate others, and provide direction amidst chaos, ambiguity, and fear.

During such times, leaders must demonstrate strong decision-making skills, focusing on problem-solving and taking decisive actions to address the crisis at hand. They should be able to assess risks, evaluate available information, and quickly adapt to changing circumstances. This involves making tough choices, sometimes with limited information, in order to minimize damage and maintain continuity.

In addition to decision-making, effective crisis leadership involves clear and concise communication. Leaders must be transparent, open, and honest with their teams or constituents, sharing vital information, addressing concerns, and providing reassurance. Strong communication helps to build trust and confidence, ensuring that everyone is on the same page and working towards a common goal.

Leaders in times of crisis must also exhibit resilience and the ability to manage their emotions. They should remain calm under pressure, displaying a level-headed approach that allows them to think clearly and creatively. By maintaining composure, leaders can inspire confidence and provide stability during uncertain and stressful periods.

Furthermore, crisis leadership involves being empathetic and supportive towards others. Leaders must be attuned to the emotional needs of their team members or followers, understanding the impact the crisis may have on their well-being. Offering support, showing empathy, and providing resources can help maintain morale and foster a sense of unity and resilience within the group.

Overall, effective leadership in times of crisis and uncertainty involves a combination of astute decision-making, clear communication, resilience, and empathy. By exhibiting these qualities, leaders can guide their organizations or teams through difficult situations, inspire confidence, and contribute to the overall success and well-being of those they lead.

This comprehensive guide provides actionable insights for leaders at all levels, equipping them to thrive in challenging times.

CHAPTER ONE

Understanding leadership in times of Crisis and Uncertainty

Leadership in times of crisis and uncertainty is a multifaceted and dynamic concept that encompasses various key elements. Understanding the nuances of leadership in such challenging circumstances is crucial for effectively navigating the complexities that arise.

Leaders often grapple with the challenge of balancing short-term demands with long-term goals, navigating ambiguity, and making decisions amid incomplete information. Uncertainties like economic fluctuations, global events, and internal dynamics can complicate strategic planning. Additionally, managing diverse teams and addressing unexpected crises demands adaptability and effective communication. The pressure to meet expectations while embracing uncertainty is a constant balancing act for leaders. Some of the essential aspects of leadership in times of crisis and uncertainty are as follows:

1. Vision and Strategy: Effective leadership in crisis situations requires a clear vision for the future and a well-defined strategy to navigate through the challenges. Leaders must be able to articulate a compelling vision that inspires confidence and provides a sense of direction even amidst uncertainty. In formulating a strategy, they should consider the broader implications of their decisions and the potential long-term impact on the organization and its stakeholders.

2. Emotional Intelligence and Empathy: Leaders need to demonstrate high levels of emotional intelligence and empathy when dealing with their teams and stakeholders during times of crisis. Understanding and addressing the fears, concerns, and anxieties of others is essential for maintaining morale and fostering a sense of togetherness. Empathetic leadership can significantly contribute to building trust and resilience within the team.

3. Decision-Making and Adaptability: Crisis situations often necessitate quick and well-informed decision-making. Leaders must be able to gather relevant information, analyze the situation, and make decisions that prioritize the well-being of their teams and the organization. Moreover, leaders must remain adaptable, as the dynamics of a crisis can change rapidly, requiring them to adjust strategies and tactics accordingly.

4. Communication and Transparency: Open and transparent communication is paramount in times of crisis. Leaders should be proactive in disseminating information, providing regular updates, and being honest about the challenges the organization faces. Transparent communication builds trust, reduces uncertainty, and enables the team to align and work towards a common goal.

5. Resilience and Optimism: Leaders must exhibit resilience and a positive outlook, even when faced with adversity. Their ability to remain steady, maintain composure, and instill hope can have a significant impact on the morale of their teams. Optimistic leadership, coupled with a belief in the organization's ability to overcome challenges, can inspire confidence and motivation.

6. Collaboration and Team Empowerment: In times of crisis, leaders should foster a collaborative environment where team members are encouraged to contribute ideas, offer solutions, and feel empowered to take on additional responsibilities. Building a strong, cohesive team that collaborates effectively can enhance problem-solving capabilities and bolster overall resilience.

7. Learning and Reflection: Effective crisis leadership involves a commitment to ongoing learning and reflection. Leaders should examine the outcomes of their decisions, take stock of

lessons learned, and apply these insights to future challenges. Continual reflection and adaptation based on experiences can enhance a leader's ability to navigate future uncertainties.

Understanding these aspects of leadership in times of crisis and uncertainty is crucial for current and aspiring leaders. By embracing these principles, leaders can better prepare themselves to navigate through tumultuous times, inspire their teams, and steer their organizations towards a positive and resilient future.

Definition of Leader, Leadership, Crisis and Uncertainty

- Leader: A leader is an individual who guides, directs, and influences a group of people towards a common goal. A leader possesses qualities such as vision, communication skills, decision-making ability, and the ability to motivate and inspire others.

- Leadership: Leadership is the act or process of directing and influencing individuals or a group towards achieving a shared goal. It involves setting a vision, motivating and inspiring others, making decisions, and coordinating and organizing resources to achieve objectives.

- Crisis: A crisis refers to a critical or unstable situation or event that poses a threat, challenge, or disruption to individuals, organizations, or society as a whole. It is characterized by a sense of urgency, uncertainty, and the potential for negative consequences or harm.

- Uncertainty: Uncertainty refers to a lack of predictability, clarity, or knowledge about the future or a particular situation. It includes the absence of reliable information or the presence of multiple potential outcomes or scenarios. Uncertainty can create challenges and difficulties in decision-making and planning.

IMPORTANCE OF LEADERSHIP IN CRISIS SITUATION

The importance of leadership in a crisis situation cannot be overstated. Effectively navigating and managing a crisis hinges on the presence of strong, capable leadership. Some key aspects that highlight the significance of leadership in a crisis situation are underlined below:

1. Decision-making: In times of crisis, rapid and well-informed decision-making is essential. Effective leaders possess the ability to process information quickly, assess risks, and make decisive choices that can steer the organization through the crisis. Their judgment and strategic thinking can significantly impact the outcome and the organization's ability to recover.

2. Communication: Clear, transparent communication is pivotal during a crisis. Leaders play a critical role in disseminating information, providing guidance, and maintaining an open line of communication with all stakeholders. Effective communication fosters trust, minimizes confusion, and ensures that everyone is aligned in their understanding of the situation and the steps being taken to address it.

3. Inspiration and Motivation: A strong leader can inspire and motivate their team to remain resilient

and focused during difficult times. By embodying optimism and confidence, leaders can instill a sense of purpose and determination within their teams, driving them to work towards solutions and maintain a positive outlook.

4. Strategic Planning and Adaptability: Leaders must be adept at developing and implementing strategic plans that address the immediate challenges posed by the crisis and also consider the long-term implications. Additionally, the ability to adapt and pivot in response to changing circumstances is crucial. Effective leaders can adjust strategies and tactics to meet evolving needs and scenarios.

5. Stakeholder Management: Leaders are responsible for managing various stakeholders, including employees, customers, suppliers, and the broader community. Their ability to balance the needs and expectations of these stakeholders, while making decisions that prioritize the organization's survival and well-being, is vital in a crisis.

6. Crisis Response Coordination: Leadership is essential in coordinating the organization's response to a crisis. This involves mobilizing resources, delegating responsibilities, and ensuring that everyone is working cohesively towards common objectives. Effective leadership can

streamline the crisis response, minimizing confusion and maximizing efficiency.

7. Building Resilience and Learning: Leaders play a crucial role in fostering resilience within the organization. They can promote a culture of learning from the crisis, using the experience to improve processes, identify vulnerabilities, and implement measures to mitigate future risks.

8. Empathy and Support: In times of crisis, leaders must demonstrate empathy, compassion, and a genuine concern for the well-being of their team members. By providing emotional support and understanding, leaders can help alleviate anxiety and stress, ultimately contributing to a more cohesive and productive team.

These aspects collectively emphasize the critical importance of leadership in a crisis situation. Effective leadership can make the difference between an organization floundering in the face of adversity and emerging stronger and more resilient. Therefore, developing leadership capabilities and preparedness for crisis management is a fundamental part of ensuring organizational success and longevity.

CHAPTER TWO

Characteristics of Effective Leaders in Times of Crisis

Effective leadership is dynamic and context-dependent, requiring leaders to adapt their approaches based on the needs of the situation and the individuals they lead. It involves a continuous process of self-improvement, learning, and the ability to inspire and guide others toward shared success. It also embodies a combination of skills, qualities, and behaviors that contribute to the success of individuals, teams, and organizations. These under listed characteristics are integral to effective leadership:

Clear Communication:

Clear communication is the foundation of effective leadership. It ensures that information is conveyed transparently, reducing misunderstandings and fostering trust within the team.

Actions:
- Provide information in a concise and understandable manner.
- Encourage open communication channels for team members.
- Actively listen to feedback and address concerns promptly.

Decisiveness:

Decisiveness is crucial for leaders to navigate challenges confidently. It involves making timely decisions based on available information, providing a sense of direction to the team.

Actions:
- Assess situations quickly and make informed decisions.
- Prioritize tasks and allocate resources effectively.
- Communicate decisions clearly and confidently.

Empathy and Emotional Intelligence:

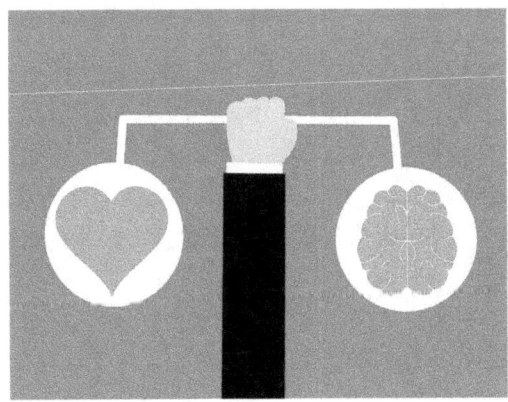

Empathy and emotional intelligence are essential for understanding and connecting with team members. They contribute to a positive work environment and strengthen interpersonal relationships.

Actions:
- Demonstrate understanding of others' perspectives and emotions.
- Actively listen to team members and show genuine concern.
- Navigate conflicts with empathy and seek mutually beneficial resolutions.

Adaptability and Flexibility:

Adaptability and flexibility are vital in dynamic work environments. Leaders who embrace change and encourage a flexible mindset can effectively navigate evolving circumstances.

Actions:
- Be open to new ideas and approaches.
- Adjust strategies and plans based on changing situations.
- Foster a culture that values continuous learning and adaptability.

Accountability and Responsibility:

Accountability and responsibility ensure that leaders and team members take ownership of their actions and decisions. They contribute to a culture of trust and reliability.

Actions:
- Clearly define roles and expectations within the team.
- Hold oneself and team members accountable for their contributions.
- Admit mistakes, take corrective actions, and learn from experiences.

These characteristics collectively define a well-rounded and effective leader. By embodying clear communication, decisiveness, empathy, adaptability, and accountability, leaders can inspire confidence, foster collaboration, and navigate challenges with resilience and integrity.

CHAPTER THREE

Strategies for Leading in Times of Crisis and Uncertainty

Creating a Vision and Setting Priorities

In times of crisis and uncertainty, creating a vision and setting priorities becomes even more crucial. A clear and inspiring vision can provide a sense of direction and hope amid turmoil, while setting priorities helps focus efforts on critical activities that address immediate challenges and pave the way for long-term resilience. Effective leadership in such times involves communicating a compelling vision and swiftly identifying and prioritizing actions that align with the vision, guiding the team through the crisis towards a brighter future.

Great Leaders often;
- Communicate their vision to inspire and provide direction:

A good leader communicates their vision effectively by:

1. **Clarity**: Clearly articulating the vision, ensuring that everyone understands the goals and objectives.

2. **Passion**: Expressing enthusiasm and passion for the vision to inspire and energize the team.

3. **Consistency**: Repeating the vision consistently to reinforce its importance and keep it at the forefront of everyone's minds.

4. **Visualizations:** Using vivid and compelling visuals to help team members visualize the desired outcome.

5. **Storytelling:** Crafting stories that connect with the vision, making it relatable and memorable for the team.

6. **Inclusivity:** Involving team members in discussions about the vision, fostering a sense of ownership and commitment.

7. **Listening:** Actively listening to team members' perspectives and incorporating valuable insights into the vision.

8. **Leading by Example:** Demonstrating behaviors and actions aligned with the vision, setting a standard for others to follow.

By employing these communication strategies, a good leader creates a shared understanding and sense of purpose, fostering a motivated and aligned team.

- Empower the team to take decisive actions aligned with the vision:

A leader can empower their team by fostering a culture of open communication and trust. Clearly communicate the vision, provide autonomy within defined boundaries, encourage diverse perspectives, and recognize and celebrate decisive actions that align with the shared vision. This helps build a sense of ownership and commitment within the team.

Identify critical priorities and focus on immediate challenges. A leader can identify critical priorities and focus on immediate challenges by:

1. **Setting Clear Goals:** Clearly define short-term and long-term goals aligned with the overall vision.

2. **Assessing Impact:** Prioritize tasks based on their potential impact on the team's objectives and the organization's overall success.

3. **Risk Assessment:** Evaluate potential risks and urgency associated with each task to determine immediate challenges.

4. **Leveraging Team Input:** Seek input from team members to gain diverse perspectives and identify critical priorities collaboratively.

5. **Time Management:** Allocate time efficiently, ensuring that urgent and high-impact tasks receive appropriate attention.

6. **Flexibility:** Stay adaptable and be willing to adjust priorities based on changing circumstances or emerging issues.

By combining these approaches, a leader can effectively identify and address critical priorities and immediate challenges, ensuring focused and strategic leadership.

- Stay agile and adaptable to meet changing circumstances:

A leader stays agile and adaptable by cultivating a growth mindset, embracing change, and encouraging a flexible team culture. Regularly reassess goals and strategies, seek diverse perspectives, and stay informed about industry trends. Foster a collaborative environment where experimentation and learning from setbacks are valued. Continuous self-reflection and a willingness to adjust plans based on evolving circumstances are essential for staying agile as a leader.

Building Strong Teams and Trust

A leader should aim to build a cohesive and high-performing team with the following characteristics:

1. **Clear Purpose and Goals:**
Clearly articulate the team's mission and objectives. For instance, a software development team may have a goal to deliver a cutting-edge product within a specified timeframe.

2. **Diverse Skill Set:**
Assemble a team with a variety of skills relevant to the project. In a marketing team, this could include individuals skilled in content creation, analytics, and social media management.

3. Open Communication:

Encourage regular team meetings, open forums for discussions, and feedback sessions. A leader might implement a communication platform to facilitate transparent and instant communication.

4. Trust and Collaboration:

Build trust by assigning responsibilities based on team members' strengths. Foster collaboration through team-building activities, workshops, or collaborative project work.

5. Adaptability and Flexibility:

In a rapidly changing industry, like technology, the team should be adaptable to new tools and methodologies. A leader might encourage continuous learning and provide resources for skill development.

6. Shared Values:

Establish a set of core values that guide the team's behavior. For instance, if innovation is a value, the team might allocate time for brainstorming sessions or experimentation.

7. Recognition and Celebration:

Acknowledge individual and team achievements. This could be as simple as a shout-out in a team meeting or a more formal recognition program.

8. Empowerment:

Delegate responsibilities and empower team members to make decisions within their areas of expertise. This not only builds trust but also fosters a sense of ownership.

9. Continuous Improvement:

Instill a culture of continuous improvement by regularly assessing team processes and seeking feedback. This could involve retrospectives after projects to identify areas for enhancement.

10. Resilience:

Encourage resilience in the face of challenges. Share stories of overcoming obstacles and emphasize the importance of learning from setbacks rather than dwelling on failures.

Building such a team requires time, dedication, and a commitment to cultivating a positive and collaborative work environment.

Managing Risk and Making Tough Decisions

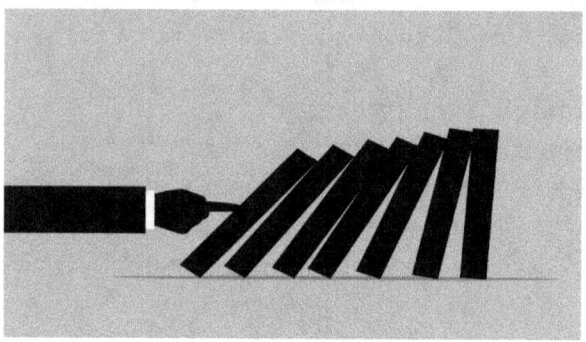

Managing risk and making tough decisions are integral parts of leadership. Here's a breakdown:

Managing Risk
1. Risk Assessment:
   - Identify potential risks and assess their impact on the project or organization. For example, in a product launch, risks could include market fluctuations or technical issues.

2. Risk Mitigation:
   - Develop strategies to mitigate identified risks. This might involve creating contingency plans, diversifying resources, or implementing preventive measures.

3. Data-Informed Decision Making:
- Use data to inform risk management decisions. Analyze relevant metrics and market trends to anticipate potential challenges.

4. Cross-Functional Collaboration:
- Involve key stakeholders and experts from various departments to gain diverse perspectives on potential risks. This collaborative approach enhances risk identification and mitigation.

5. Adaptability:
- Foster a culture of adaptability. Teams should be prepared to adjust strategies based on emerging risks and changing circumstances.

Making Tough Decisions
1. Clarity of Values:
- Align decisions with core values and organizational mission. This ensures that tough choices are in line with the overall purpose.

2. Consideration of Stakeholders:
- Evaluate how decisions impact various stakeholders. In a workforce reduction scenario, for instance, consider the well-being of employees, while also addressing the financial health of the organization.

3. Data-Driven Decision Making:

- Collect and analyze relevant data to support decision-making. This could include financial projections, market research, or performance metrics.

4. Risk vs. Reward Analysis:

- Assess potential risks and rewards associated with each decision. Understanding the balance helps in making informed choices.

5. Timely Decision Making:

- Avoid prolonged indecision. While careful consideration is essential, timely decision-making is crucial to prevent stagnation.

6. Transparent Communication:

- Clearly communicate the reasons behind tough decisions to the team. Transparency fosters trust, even when the decisions are challenging.

7. Learn from Decisions:

- Treat decisions, especially tough ones, as learning opportunities. Evaluate outcomes, gather feedback, and use the experience to enhance future decision-making processes.

8. Emotional Intelligence:

- Be aware of the emotional impact of decisions on yourself and others. Leaders with high emotional intelligence can navigate tough decisions with empathy and resilience.

9. Seeking Counsel:
- Consult with mentors, advisors, or experienced colleagues when facing particularly challenging decisions. External perspectives can provide valuable insights.

10. Ownership of Decisions:
- Take ownership of decisions, whether they lead to success or challenges. This builds credibility and encourages accountability within the team.

Leadership often involves striking a balance between managing risks effectively and making tough decisions that propel the organization forward. Both skills are refined through experience, self-reflection, and a commitment to continual improvement.

Maintaining Calm and Reducing Anxiety

Maintaining calm and reducing anxiety in leadership is crucial for effective decision-making and team well-being. Here's how:

1. **Mindfulness Practices:**
   - Incorporate mindfulness techniques such as deep breathing or meditation into your routine to stay grounded and focused during stressful situations.

2. **Effective Time Management:**
   - Prioritize tasks and manage time efficiently to avoid feeling overwhelmed. Breaking down larger tasks into smaller, manageable steps can reduce anxiety.

3. **Delegation:**
   - Delegate responsibilities to trusted team members, promoting a sense of shared ownership and reducing the burden on individual leaders.

4. **Clear Communication:**
   - Communicate openly with your team about challenges and plans. Transparent communication fosters a supportive environment and minimizes uncertainty.

5. **Support System:**
   - Build a strong support system, both within and outside the organization. Discussing concerns with mentors, colleagues, or friends can provide valuable perspectives.

6. Balanced Work-Life Integration:

- Strive for a healthy work-life balance. Ensure that personal time and self-care are integrated into your schedule to prevent burnout.

7. Flexibility and Adaptability:

- Embrace flexibility and adaptability in your leadership approach. Being open to change reduces anxiety associated with unexpected challenges.

8. Problem-Solving Mindset:

- Cultivate a problem-solving mindset. Instead of dwelling on problems, focus on finding solutions. This proactive approach can alleviate anxiety.

9. Regular Breaks:

- Take regular breaks during the workday to recharge. Physical activity, even a short walk, can positively impact mood and reduce stress.

10. Continuous Learning:

- Stay informed about leadership strategies and industry trends. Continuous learning builds confidence and reduces anxiety about navigating unknown territories.

11. Celebrate Achievements:

- Acknowledge and celebrate both personal and team achievements. Positive reinforcement boosts morale and contributes to a more positive work environment.

12. Set Realistic Expectations:
- Establish realistic expectations for yourself and your team. Unrealistic goals can lead to unnecessary stress and anxiety.

13. Seek Professional Help:
- If anxiety becomes overwhelming, consider seeking professional guidance. A counselor or mental health professional can provide valuable support and coping strategies.

Remember, being a calm and composed leader doesn't mean avoiding challenges; it means navigating them with resilience and a clear mindset. Prioritize self-care and create a work environment that promotes the well-being of both you and your team.

Emphasizing Transparency and Honesty

Emphasizing transparency and honesty in leadership is essential for building trust and fostering a positive organizational culture. Here's how you can prioritize these values:

1. Open Communication:
- Foster an environment where open communication is encouraged. Share information regarding organizational goals, challenges, and decision-making processes.

2. Clear Expectations:
- Clearly communicate expectations for the team. Transparency in setting goals and expectations promotes a shared understanding of objectives.

3. Honest Feedback:
- Provide honest and constructive feedback to team members. This contributes to their professional growth and reinforces a culture of transparency.

4. Share Decision-Making Rationale:
- When making significant decisions, communicate the rationale behind them. Understanding the reasoning fosters trust and helps team members align with organizational goals.

5. Admitting Mistakes:
- Be willing to admit when you or the organization has made a mistake. Acknowledging errors demonstrates humility and reinforces the importance of honesty.

6. Consistent Messaging:
   - Ensure consistency in messaging. Align verbal communication with actions to avoid confusion and maintain credibility.

7. Accessibility:
   - Be accessible to team members. Approachability promotes open conversations and encourages individuals to share concerns or ideas without fear of reprisal.

8. Transparency in Processes:
   - Clearly outline processes and procedures within the organization. Understanding how things work promotes a sense of security and trust.

9. Ethical Decision-Making:
   - Make decisions based on ethical considerations. Upholding high ethical standards reinforces trust among team members and stakeholders.

10. Share Successes and Failures:
   - Celebrate successes openly, and also discuss failures as opportunities for learning. Sharing both sides of the coin promotes honesty about the organization's journey.

11. Encourage Employee Feedback:
   - Create mechanisms for employees to provide feedback. Act on constructive criticism,

demonstrating a commitment to improvement and transparency.

12. **Transparency in Resource Allocation:**
   - Clearly communicate how resources are allocated within the organization. This could include budgeting, project assignments, or opportunities for professional development.

13. **Lead by Example:**
   - Demonstrate transparency and honesty in your own actions. Leaders who lead by example set the tone for the entire organization.

14. **Training on Transparency:**
   - Provide training or workshops on the importance of transparency and honesty. Help employees understand how these values contribute to a healthy work environment.

By consistently prioritizing transparency and honesty, leaders can build a foundation of trust, enhance employee engagement, and create a positive organizational culture.

CHAPTER FOUR

Case Studies of Effective Leadership in Times of Crisis and Uncertainty

Successful Leadership during Natural Disasters

Here are two case studies illustrating successful leadership during natural disasters:

1. Hurricane Katrina (2005) - Mayor Rudy Giuliani, New York City

- **Situation:** Although not directly impacted by Hurricane Katrina, Mayor Giuliani provided support and resources to the affected areas, particularly New Orleans.

- **Leadership Response:**
- **Swift Action:** Mayor Giuliani acted quickly, mobilizing emergency response teams and sending supplies and personnel to assist with the relief efforts in New Orleans.
- **Clear Communication:** He communicated effectively with the public, providing updates on the city's contributions and encouraging citizens to support the relief efforts.
- **Coordination with Agencies:** Giuliani worked collaboratively with federal, state, and local agencies to ensure a coordinated response.
- **Outcome:**
- New York City's proactive assistance and Giuliani's leadership demonstrated solidarity and contributed significantly to the relief efforts in the aftermath of Hurricane Katrina.

2. Earthquake in Japan (2011) - Prime Minister Naoto Kan:

- **Situation:** A massive earthquake and tsunami struck Japan, leading to nuclear reactor meltdowns and a complex crisis.
- **Leadership Response:**
- **Decisive Decision-Making:** Prime Minister Kan made decisive decisions, including initiating evacuation plans and coordinating international assistance.
- **Open Communication:** Kan maintained transparent communication, providing regular updates to the public and international community on the evolving situation.
- **Coordination and Collaboration:** The Japanese government collaborated with international organizations and sought assistance from countries with expertise in nuclear energy.
- **Outcome:**
- Prime Minister Kan's leadership during the crisis received international recognition. His decisive actions and open communication contributed to effective disaster response and recovery efforts.

These case studies highlight successful leadership during natural disasters, showcasing qualities such as swift action, clear communication, collaboration, and decisive decision-making. Leaders who prioritize coordination and transparency can significantly impact the outcomes of relief and recovery efforts in the aftermath of natural disasters.

Leadership in Financial Crises

Let us look at two case studies illustrating leadership during financial crises:

1. 2008 Global Financial Crisis - Ben Bernanke, Chairman of the Federal Reserve:**

- **Situation:** The collapse of major financial institutions and the housing market crash triggered a global financial crisis in 2008.

- **Leadership Response:**

- **Swift Intervention:** Bernanke led the Federal Reserve in implementing unconventional monetary policies, including bailouts and interest rate cuts, to stabilize the financial system.

- **Transparency:** He communicated transparently about the severity of the crisis and the steps being taken to address it, fostering confidence in the financial markets.

- **Collaboration:** Bernanke collaborated with international central banks and policymakers to coordinate a global response to the crisis.
- **Outcome:**
- Bernanke's leadership played a pivotal role in preventing a complete financial collapse. The U.S. economy eventually stabilized, and reforms were implemented to prevent a similar crisis in the future.

2. Asian Financial Crisis (1997-1998) - Mahathir Mohamad, Prime Minister of Malaysia:
- **Situation:** The crisis involved currency devaluations, economic downturns, and financial instability in several Asian countries.
- **Leadership Response:**
- **Capital Controls:** Mahathir implemented capital controls to stabilize the Malaysian currency and prevent further economic deterioration.
- **Government Intervention:** The government took control of troubled financial institutions, injecting funds and restructuring the banking sector.
- **Economic Diversification:** Mahathir focused on diversifying Malaysia's economy to reduce dependence on external factors and strengthen resilience.
- **Outcome:**
- Malaysia recovered relatively quickly compared to other affected nations. Mahathir's decisive actions, including unconventional economic measures, contributed to the country's resilience during the crisis.

These case studies highlight effective leadership during financial crises, emphasizing qualities such as swift intervention, transparency, collaboration, and decisive decision-making. Leaders who navigate financial turmoil with a strategic and coordinated approach can mitigate the impact and set the foundation for recovery.

Leadership in Public Health Emergencies

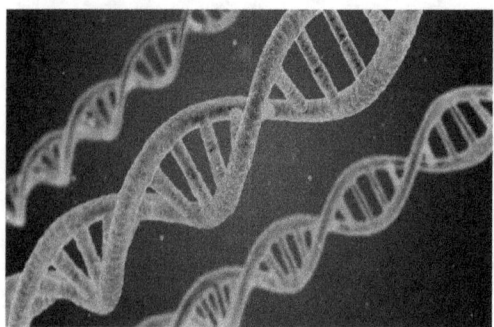

Two case studies illustrating leadership during public health emergencies;

1. Ebola Outbreak (2014-2016) - Dr. Joanne Liu, Médecins Sans Frontières (MSF):
   - **Situation:** The Ebola virus outbreak in West Africa posed a significant public health threat,

leading to widespread panic and a strained healthcare system.

- **Leadership Response:**
- **Frontline Action:** MSF, under Dr. Liu's leadership, deployed medical teams to the epicenter of the outbreak, providing crucial healthcare services and contributing to the containment efforts.
- **Advocacy for Global Response:** Dr. Liu advocated for a stronger global response, urging governments and international organizations to commit resources and personnel to address the crisis.
- **Transparency:** MSF openly communicated about the challenges faced on the ground, raising awareness about the severity of the outbreak.
- **Outcome:**
- Dr. Liu's leadership and MSF's proactive involvement played a crucial role in containing the Ebola outbreak. Their efforts underscored the importance of immediate and robust action in public health emergencies.

2. COVID-19 Pandemic (ongoing) - Dr. Anthony Fauci, Director of the National Institute of Allergy and Infectious Diseases (NIAID):
- **Situation:** The global COVID-19 pandemic presented an unprecedented public health challenge with widespread health, economic, and social implications.

- **Leadership Response:**
  - **Scientific Expertise:** Dr. Fauci provided consistent, evidence-based guidance and expertise, becoming a trusted source of information for the public and policymakers.
  - **Communication:** He maintained clear and transparent communication, updating the public on the evolving situation, preventive measures, and vaccine development progress.
  - **Collaboration:** Dr. Fauci collaborated with international health organizations, researchers, and pharmaceutical companies to accelerate vaccine development and distribution.
- **Outcome:**
  - Dr. Fauci's leadership contributed to informed decision-making and coordinated efforts in responding to the pandemic. His advocacy for science-driven responses underscored the importance of relying on experts during public health crises.

These case studies highlight effective leadership in public health emergencies, emphasizing qualities such as rapid response, scientific expertise, transparent communication, and collaboration. Leaders who prioritize evidence-based strategies and foster international cooperation play a crucial role in managing and mitigating the impact of public health crises.

CHAPTER FIVE

Developing Leadership Skills for Crisis Situations

Self-awareness and Self-reflection

Leaders can demonstrate self-awareness and self-reflection through various actions and behaviors:

1. Seeking Feedback:
   - Actively seek feedback from peers, team members, and mentors. Leaders who genuinely

want to understand how they are perceived demonstrate a commitment to self-awareness.

2. Regular Self-Assessment:
   - Set aside time for regular self-assessment. Reflect on your actions, decisions, and interactions with others. Consider how your behavior aligns with your values and goals.

3. Acknowledging Mistakes:
   - Admitting mistakes openly and taking responsibility demonstrates humility and self-awareness. Leaders who learn from their errors contribute to a culture of continuous improvement.

4. Embracing Constructive Criticism:
   - Welcome constructive criticism and view it as an opportunity for growth. Leaders who value feedback from others show a willingness to evolve and refine their leadership style.

5. Journaling:
   - Maintain a leadership journal to document thoughts, challenges, and lessons learned. Writing can be a powerful tool for self-reflection and gaining insights into your leadership journey.

6. 360-Degree Assessments:
   - Participate in 360-degree assessments where feedback is gathered from peers, subordinates, and superiors. This comprehensive approach provides

a well-rounded view of leadership strengths and areas for improvement.

7. Mindfulness Practices:

- Engage in mindfulness practices, such as meditation or deep breathing exercises, to enhance self-awareness. These practices can help leaders stay present and attuned to their thoughts and emotions.

8. Regular Check-Ins with Yourself:

- Schedule regular check-ins with yourself to evaluate your overall well-being, stress levels, and work-life balance. Self-aware leaders understand the importance of maintaining personal health and balance.

9. Attending Leadership Development Programs:

- Participate in leadership development programs or workshops that focus on self-awareness and self-reflection. These programs often provide tools and frameworks for personal growth.

10. Encouraging Open Dialogue:

- Build a culture of open interaction within your team. Encouraging team members to provide honest feedback creates an environment where self-awareness is valued.

11. Setting Personal Goals:

- Establish and revisit personal development goals regularly. Leaders who set specific, measurable, and achievable goals demonstrate a commitment to continuous improvement.

12. Empathy and Active Listening:

- Practice empathy and active listening. A crucial component of self-awareness is emotional intelligence, which is demonstrated by leaders who truly comprehend and relate to people.

13. Engaging in Coaching or Mentoring:

- Seek out coaching or mentoring relationships where you can receive guidance and insights from experienced individuals. External perspectives can enhance self-awareness.

14. Adapting Leadership Style:

- Be flexible in adapting your leadership style based on the needs of the situation and the team. Leaders who recognize the impact of their style on different contexts demonstrate self-awareness.

By consistently demonstrating these behaviors, leaders not only showcase self-awareness and self-reflection but also contribute to the development of a positive and growth-oriented organizational culture.

Continual Learning and Adaptation

Continual learning and adaptation are cornerstones of effective leadership. Leaders can integrate these principles into their leadership approach. Here's how:

1. **Curiosity and Open-Mindedness:**
   - Cultivate a curious and open mindset. Embrace new ideas, perspectives, and approaches, fostering a culture of curiosity within the team.

2. **Regular Skill Assessments:**
   - Periodically assess your skills and identify areas for improvement. Leaders who continuously refine their skill set remain adaptable in dynamic environments.

3. **Stay Informed About Industry Trends:**
   - Keep abreast of industry trends, technological advancements, and market changes. Staying informed enables leaders to make informed decisions and adapt strategies accordingly.

4. **Learning from Setbacks:**
   - View setbacks as learning opportunities. Analyze failures, extract lessons, and apply newfound insights to enhance future decision-making and problem-solving.

5. **Invest in Professional Development:**
   - Allocate time and resources for professional development. Attend workshops, conferences, and training programs to stay current with evolving best practices and leadership methodologies.

6. **Encourage a Learning Culture:**
   - Foster a culture of continuous learning within your team. Encourage team members to pursue further education, attend relevant training, and share knowledge with one another.

7. **Adaptability in Leadership Style:**
   - Recognize that different situations may require different leadership styles. Leaders who can adapt their approaches to fit the context are more likely to inspire and guide their teams effectively.

8. **Seek Feedback and Constructive Criticism:**
   - Regularly seek feedback from peers, team members, and mentors. Constructive criticism provides valuable insights and helps leaders adjust their strategies and behaviors.

9. **Experimentation and Innovation:**
   - Encourage a culture of experimentation and innovation. Leaders who are open to trying new approaches foster creativity and adaptability within their teams.

10. Networking and Collaboration:
- Build a strong professional network. Collaborate with peers and industry professionals, as diverse perspectives can provide fresh insights and solutions to challenges.

11. Set Personal Learning Goals:
- Establish personal learning goals and regularly assess progress. Setting measurable objectives helps leaders stay focused on continual improvement.

12. Reflect on Experiences:
- Regularly reflect on past experiences, both successes, and failures. Extracting lessons from these experiences contributes to continual learning and helps refine decision-making.

13. Embrace Technology:
- Stay current with technological advancements relevant to your field. Technological literacy allows leaders to leverage innovations for organizational success.

14. Mentorship and Coaching:
- Engage in mentorship or coaching relationships. Learning from experienced individuals provides valuable guidance and accelerates personal and professional development.

By incorporating these practices, leaders can foster a culture of continual learning and adaptation, ensuring they remain agile, resilient, and well-equipped to lead effectively in an ever-changing environment.

Building Resilience

Building resilience in leadership is essential for navigating challenges and maintaining effectiveness in the face of adversity. Key strategies to enhance resilience includes:

1. **Develop a Growth Mindset:**
   - Cultivate a growth mindset that views challenges as opportunities for learning and growth. Embrace setbacks as part of the leadership journey.

2. **Strengthen Emotional Intelligence:**
   - Enhance emotional intelligence to understand and manage emotions effectively. Leaders with high emotional intelligence can navigate stressful situations and maintain composure.

3. **Build a Support Network:**
   - Foster strong connections with mentors, colleagues, and friends. A robust support network

provides encouragement and different perspectives during challenging times.

4. Self-Care and Well-Being:
   - Prioritize self-care to maintain physical and mental well-being. Regular exercise, adequate sleep, and mindfulness practices contribute to overall resilience.

5. Set Realistic Expectations:
   - Establish realistic expectations for yourself and your team. Unrealistic goals can lead to unnecessary stress and hinder resilience.

6. Adaptability and Flexibility:
   - Cultivate adaptability and flexibility in your leadership approach. Be open to change and adjust strategies based on evolving circumstances.

7. Learn from Adversity:
   - View challenges as opportunities for learning. Reflect on past difficulties, extract valuable lessons, and apply them to future situations.

8. Effective Time Management:
   - Develop strong time management skills to prioritize tasks and avoid burnout. Efficient use of time contributes to maintaining resilience in demanding situations.

9. Positive Mindset:

- Foster a positive mindset by focusing on strengths and solutions. Positivity not only improves your outlook but also influences the morale of your team.

10. Encourage Open Communication:

- Create an environment where open communication is maintained. A culture of transparency fosters trust and enables teams to navigate challenges collaboratively.

11. Problem-Solving Skills:

- Strengthen problem-solving skills to address challenges systematically. A proactive approach to problem-solving enhances resilience and minimizes the impact of obstacles.

12. Continuous Learning:

- Leaders who stay curious and seek knowledge are better equipped to adapt to new situations.

13. Celebrate Achievements:

- Acknowledge and celebrate both personal and team achievements. Recognizing successes contributes to a positive work environment and boosts morale.

14. Crisis Preparedness:
- Develop crisis response plans to be prepared for unforeseen challenges. A proactive approach to crisis management enhances overall resilience.

15. Mindfulness and Stress Reduction:
- Integrate mindfulness practices and stress reduction techniques into your routine. Mindfulness enhances self-awareness and promotes a calm and focused mindset.

16. Delegate Effectively:
- Delegate tasks to distribute responsibilities and prevent overload. Effective delegation empowers team members and lightens the leadership burden.

17. Seek Professional Support:
- If needed, seek support from a mentor, coach, or mental health professional. Having an external perspective can provide valuable insights and guidance.

Building resilience is an ongoing process that requires intentional effort and a commitment to personal and professional development. By incorporating these strategies, leaders can navigate challenges with strength and adaptability, inspiring resilience in themselves and their teams.

Seeking Feedback and Mentorship

Seeking feedback and mentorship are valuable practices for personal and professional development in leadership. Here's how you can effectively integrate these elements into your leadership journey:

Seeking Feedback

1. Create a Feedback Culture:
   - Foster an environment where open and constructive feedback is encouraged. Establish a culture that values continuous improvement.

2. Specific Feedback Requests:
   - When seeking feedback, be specific about the aspects you want insights on. This helps the giver provide targeted and actionable input.

3. Regular Check-Ins:
   - Schedule regular one-on-one check-ins with team members, peers, and superiors. Regular communication provides ongoing opportunities for feedback.

4. Anonymous Feedback Mechanisms:
   - Implement anonymous feedback mechanisms, such as surveys or suggestion boxes, to encourage honest and candid feedback from team members.

5. Listen Actively:

- Actively listen to feedback without becoming defensive. Approach it as an opportunity for learning and growth.

6. Feedback on Leadership Style:

- Request feedback on your leadership style, communication, decision-making, and interpersonal skills. Understanding how others perceive your leadership is crucial.

7. Acknowledge and Act:

- Acknowledge the feedback received, whether positive or constructive. Demonstrate a commitment to improvement by taking actionable steps based on the feedback.

Mentorship:

1. Identify Potential Mentors:

- Identify individuals with experience and expertise in areas relevant to your leadership goals. Look for mentors who align with your values and aspirations.

2. Express Your Goals:

- Clearly communicate your professional and leadership goals to potential mentors. This helps them understand how they can best support your development.

3. Build Genuine Connections:
- Establish genuine connections with potential mentors. Building a strong rapport creates a foundation for meaningful mentorship.

4. Seek Diverse Perspectives:
- Consider mentors with diverse perspectives. Exposure to different viewpoints enriches your understanding and approach to leadership.

5. Regular Check-Ins:
- Schedule regular check-ins with your mentor. Use these sessions to discuss challenges, seek advice, and receive guidance on your leadership journey.

6. Learn from Their Experiences:
- Tap into your mentor's experiences and learn from their successes and failures. Extract valuable insights that can inform your own decision-making.

7. Be Open to Feedback:
- Be open to constructive feedback from your mentor. Their insights can offer valuable guidance for your leadership development.

8. Reciprocal Relationship:
- Understand that mentorship is a reciprocal relationship. Be open to offering your skills, insights, and perspectives as well.

9. **Expand Your Network:**
   - Leverage your mentor's network to broaden your professional connections. Networking opportunities facilitated by mentorship can open doors to new possibilities.

10. **Formal Mentorship Programs:**
    - Explore formal mentorship programs within your organization or professional networks. These programs often provide structured guidance and support.

By actively seeking feedback and engaging in mentorship, you can accelerate your leadership growth, gain valuable insights, and navigate challenges more effectively. These practices contribute to continuous improvement and foster a positive and supportive leadership journey.

CHAPTER SIX

Overcoming challenges and pitfalls in crisis leadership

Leadership requires strategic and thoughtful approaches to overcome challenging situations and pitfalls. Let's explore each aspect:

Managing Panic and Fear

Challenge:
During a crisis, panic and fear can spread rapidly among team members and stakeholders, affecting decision-making and overall morale.

Strategies:
- **Communication Transparency:** Provide clear and transparent communication to address concerns and uncertainties.
- **Stress the Importance of Calmness:** Emphasize the importance of remaining calm to make informed decisions.
- **Provide Reassurance:** Share a vision for overcoming challenges and highlight past successes.

Balancing Short-term and Long-term Goals

Challenge:
Balancing immediate actions with long-term goals is challenging, as the urgency of crisis situations may overshadow strategic planning.

Strategies:
- **Prioritize Critical Actions:** Identify and prioritize immediate actions that align with long-term objectives.
- **Maintain a Strategic Focus:** Continuously assess how short-term decisions contribute to long-term resilience.
- **Adapt Plans as Needed:** Be open to adjusting strategies based on evolving circumstances.

Handling Criticism and Public Pressure

Challenge:
Leaders in crisis situations often face public scrutiny and criticism, which can be challenging to manage.

Strategies:
- **Maintain Transparency:** Communicate openly about challenges and steps being taken to address them.
- **Acknowledge Concerns:** Acknowledge public concerns and demonstrate a commitment to addressing them.
- **Focus on Solutions:** Shift the narrative towards solutions and positive actions.

Maintaining Personal Well-being

Challenge:
Leaders may neglect personal well-being while managing a crisis, leading to burnout and decreased effectiveness.

Strategies:
- **Set Boundaries:** Establish clear boundaries between work and personal life to prevent burnout.
- **Delegate Responsibilities:** Delegate tasks to distribute the workload and avoid overwhelming oneself.
- **Prioritize Self-Care:** Prioritize adequate sleep, exercise, and moments of relaxation to maintain mental and physical health.

Overcoming challenges in crisis leadership requires a combination of effective communication, strategic decision-making, resilience in the face of criticism, and a commitment to personal well-being. By addressing these aspects, leaders can navigate crises more effectively and guide their teams towards successful outcomes.

CHAPTER SEVEN

The Role of Ethical Leadership in Times of Crisis

Ethical leadership plays a pivotal role in guiding organizations through times of crisis. Let's explore the key aspects:

Ethics and Values in Decision-making:

Importance:
During a crisis, decisions can have far-reaching consequences. Ethical leadership involves making choices aligned with a strong moral framework.

Actions:
- **Clarify Core Values:** Clearly articulate the organization's core values and ethical principles.
- **Evaluate Decisions Ethically:** Assess decisions against ethical standards, considering the impact on stakeholders.
- **Lead by Example:** Demonstrate ethical behavior in decision-making to set a standard for the team.

Building Trust and Credibility

Importance:
Trust is essential during a crisis. Ethical leaders build and maintain trust by consistently demonstrating honesty, integrity, and reliability.

Actions:
- **Transparent Communication:** Communicate openly about decisions, challenges, and the organization's response.
- **Consistent Behavior:** Align actions with stated values to reinforce credibility.
- **Accountability:** Take responsibility for decisions, whether they lead to success or setbacks.

Mitigating Conflicts of Interest

Challenge:
Crises can create situations where personal interests may conflict with organizational well-being. Ethical leaders actively address and mitigate such conflicts.

Strategies:
- **Establish Clear Policies:** Implement and communicate policies to address conflicts of interest.
- **Fair Decision-Making:** Ensure decisions are impartial and prioritize the organization's best interests.
- **Recusal when Necessary:** Step back from decision-making in situations where personal interests could compromise objectivity.

Ethical leadership provides a solid foundation for navigating crises with integrity, fostering a culture of trust, and making decisions that align with organizational values. By consistently upholding ethical standards, leaders contribute to the resilience and long-term success of their organizations.

CONCLUSION

In conclusion, leadership in times of crisis and uncertainty demands a multifaceted approach that combines strategic thinking, emotional intelligence, and ethical decision-making. Successful leaders not only guide their teams through challenges but also foster a resilient organizational culture that can adapt, learn, and thrive in the face of uncertainty. Remember, effective leadership in times of crisis is a dynamic and evolving journey. By incorporating these comprehensive piece of study, leaders can navigate uncertainty with confidence, inspire their teams, and contribute to the resilience and success of their organizations.